Oasis

Poems & Paintings

Oasis
Poems & Paintings

Laura Williams-Chassot

TransMedia Press
Philadelphia, PA

Cover illustration
Laura Williams-Chasot
"Oasis"
55" H x 45" W
Acrylic on canvas

ISBN 978-0-9820255-9-8

TransMedia Press is an imprint of
The TransMedia Publishing Group
Philadelphia, PA

Dedication

This work honors my brilliant and generous sister, Greta D. Morton, who was an artist, writer, and poet. It honors also, my grandmother, Carrie Porter, who wrote essays that won prizes at Rockefeller Center in New York, NY and my Aunt Marie Porter who was a great storyteller and writer of short stories. Each one left a positive impression on me.

It is dedicated to all poets who have inspired me throughout my life, especially my daughter who consistently inspires poetry whenever I speak with her!

Contents

Contents

Preface

The decision to put images and words together has given me an opportunity to work in two disciplines under one cover. Each discipline requires focus. Each communicates the nature of the artist's heart. The images presented here are not meant to illustrate a specific poem, in most cases. These images are included to reflect significant steps on my journey in the visualization of life.

I have included paintings which allow the poems to breathe, much in the way that abstract ideas and paintings allow us to step out of a box and see the space around it.

Oasis is that part of me that revives, rejuvenates, quenches and pleasures in awareness of each step taken to enjoy, *right now.* Oasis further expresses a challenging existence that yields insight, promotes spiritual growth and fosters confidence in the power of creation.

Laura Williams-Chassot

Acknowledgments

My beloved partner Emmanuel Chassot encourages and inspires my efforts to create art. He has been an invaluable resource for suggestions and help in organizing text and delivering graphics for this project. His consistent support has lifted my spirits during times of great challenges.

Also, I wish to express praise and appreciation for my dearest friend, poet, painter and photographer, Nashormeh Lindo. From the beginning she encouraged me to write poetry. She insisted that I perform my work at different venues with her and to acquire the habit of having poems with me always. This enabled me to read in places unexpectedly, making reading and performing poetry an adventurous journey.

The patience and encouragement that my publisher, Benson Fishman has exhibited in seeing this project through with me has been an extraordinary experience.

And lastly, to my family, friends and colleagues who have encouraged and supported my efforts, a very special thanks.

Introduction

Laura Williams-Chassot: And Everything in Between

Dr. Kimmika Williams-Witherspoon

Touching on everything from becoming, to notions of self, identity, growing older and posterity, Laura Williams-Chassot's work, as both a visual artist and a poet, is bold, gripping and hypnotizing.

Oasis is a new collection by Laura Williams-Chassot. Some of the pieces in this collection like In the Woods, are whimsical and melodic like a "just-made" fairy tale of old. In the Woods asks the question: What happens when a "house" shows the wear and tear of a "home" and "family" broken. And yet, even in its attention to classic, poetic notions of rhyme, rhythm and meter—the pieces are not so obscure to hide the very real, very contemporary, very timely discussions of dysfunctional families, homes and loves—that aren't always "happy-ever-after". Instead, Williams-Chassot suggests that "fairy tales" and "fantasy" are entirely two different things.

In this collection, poems like Memories, are beautiful in their simplicity. Pieces like Soul Journey: A Retrospective are ethereal and haunting and Talk of the Town is one of her more playful pieces in the text. While Life is the Sum of Choices We Make is the poetic anchor of the book because, in this collection, she has offered us a glimpse into the sum of her own life's experiences for us to take, leave or learn from.

Visually full and appealing, as an artist, she is adept at creating depth and color (see, image Under Cerulean Skies)—even when her instrument is "words" and her canvas is paper. The characters in her work—bent, cracked or bravely straight in their resolve, come to life with her words as in the piece Freedman. On the other hand, Once in a Lifetime brings back haunting memories of the tragedy of artists "gone too soon" such as Minnie Riperton or Whitney Houston.

In the suite Move: A Tragedy of Errors, the author immortalizes the memory of one of the most costly confrontations with rebelling people of color to date. In this work, Williams-Chassot provides a platform to talk candidly about dissent and the "take no prisoners" approach to lethal force sometimes waged by local governments. In pieces like Democracy, Williams-Chassot shows that she is, both a fan of the villanelle poetic form as she is of exposing injustices and costs of war. Poems like Balm in Gilead point to the ironies of politics and governments under construction.

One should note that in this collection, the paintings and the sketches are breathtaking. Larch is particularly nuanced. "Larch" is one of the visual images that spoke most poignantly to me. In that piece, a graphite drawing on paper, a woman, as a conduit of Mother Nature, adorned in foliage, stares at us—unbelieving but prayerfully, crying river tears for what we've done.

The images like Island Fantasy come alive with her work and the colors that the work calls up are infectious. Williams-Chassot's visual art, that separates each section of the text, is invocative and haunting. All of the images are vivid and layered in the story they help to tell. Her images are full and artistic—and through her work, we are drawn to the way she paints earth and nature and beauty—with and without sketchpad and paper, pen or pencil. At home in both mediums as poet/artist, rather, Laura Williams-Chassot is just as skilled an artist with her words.

The poem, also entitled The Larch is full of alliteration and onomatopoeia, and speaks passionately about the feminist/womanist view of "girl power" along with a woman's strength and beauty—throughout every stage of her life.

I have known Laura Williams-Chassot for nearly thirty years. Soft-spoken, kind at heart, wise and welcoming, she has poetically and artistically lived her life to the fullest—painting and sketching "must-see" images along the way and gathering up her words to say something real and necessary for those of us willing to listen. Laura Williams teaches "life" through her work. From her images to her words—Williams-Chassot implores her reader/audience – before it's too late, to think about birth, aging, friendship, illness, loss, death and everything in between.

Dr. Kimmika Williams-Witherspoon *is an author, playwright and performance poet, Associate Professor of Urban Theater and Community Engagement, Department of Theater, School of Theater, Film and Media Arts, Center for the Performing and Cinematic Arts, Temple University, Philadelphia, PA , USA*

Landing

Landing

How one lands, is as important as how one ascends. This stroke painting intimates a graceful and smooth descent. The warm gray background is inviting and peaceful, anchoring the movement of the contrasting gesture.

My aim is to express complex ideas with a single stroke. This is done with color choice and gestural execution. Single stroke paintings stimulate the viewer's imagination, allowing many more scenarios than depicted by the image.

One word well chosen by the poet can express a multitude of ideas.

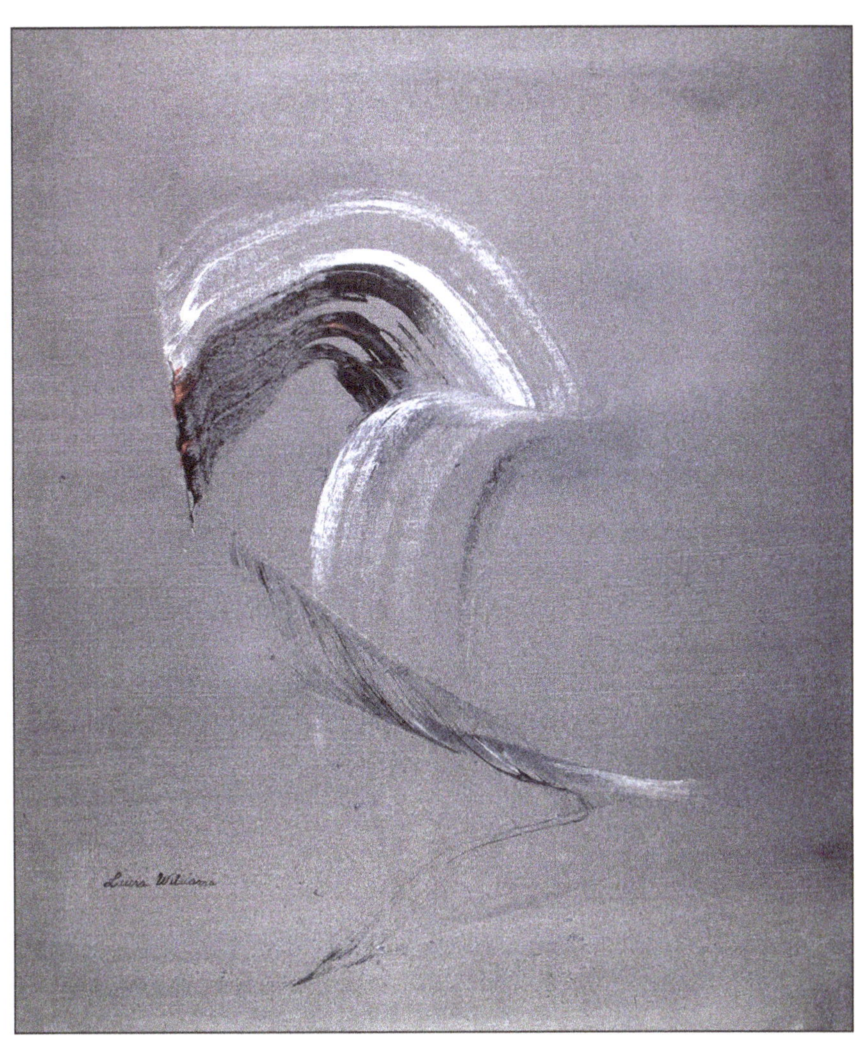

"Landing"
26″H x 23″W
Acyrlic on canvas

Beginner's Mind

I like moving in "beginner's mind".
Starting out, learning something new
Each time.
Some new discovery inspiring me
To learn more about everything I like
And in the end
I am the expert
about me!

Taste

She likes to taste crunchy and soft.

There's nothing political about it.

It's simply rhetorical wit.

Why judge her persuasion wicked or corrupt,

For who rocks to a lockstep?

You can have your cake and devour it too

It is simply up to you

To make your taste buds sing

With delightful orgasmic sighs

Try fried and crispy onion rings.

She likes to taste crunchy with soft.

Memories

The past is melting
Ice cream on a hot sidewalk where childhood skipped
Tasting mud pies crunchy and gritty
Made in red clay while playing on the hill

Finding black spiders who write in their webs
Will I die if they write my name?

The past is melting
Hot patches on flat tires
Healing pain that can't be fixed

Melting in the cauldron of Grandfather's soap
Melting in my mouth five cent candy bars

Melting memories on my tongue like butter
Butchered smells of blood
Newborn's beginning

Melting stairs descending
One potato two potato three potato four
Five potato six potato seven potato more

Life is the Sum of Choices We Make

Life is the sum of choices we make
Measured with a coffee spoon,
Whether we are sincere or fake.

Some decisions you can not shake,
One is our journey to the tomb.
Life is the sum of choices we make

Assured success we can't assume.
Anything can happen outside the womb
Whether we are sincere or fake.

We're allowed to make a mistake
Throughout it all, we can presume
Life is the sum of choices we make.

Cherish the life as we partake
While others sing a different tune,
Whether we are sincere or fake

Life is surely a piece of cake.
But there's one rule we must assume
Life is the sum of choices we make,
Whether we are sincere or fake.

Soul Journey: A Retrospect

an artist child exists
enter every form of life
and nonexistent
 nonsense
enter story
enter eye tales of dream makers
sojourners

long ago eye dreamed.
reflections manifesting
rainbows along the waters' edge of rivers
flowing over breasts of mountains
touched with fire of e-y-e
touched with fire of Eye
rainbows
speak of sun.

Key Discordant

I am key discordant
Key opening to me
Creating chaos among gods created to replace me.
I am courage
Blown up full
Creating
Puffed up
Punched out
Pushed in and pulled beyond recognition.
I
Confidence,
Evidence these truths to be
Self events
Creating my world.
I am composition.
I am compassion,
Composed.
Centered.
Love.

Artists

Make sense for us -
Make our senses real for us.
Are we computers?
Are we one and the same?
Are we chess pieces in a higher being's game?
Are we evolving and developing for some miseries name?
Make sense
Make sense real to us…

I'm a fish
A fish

Swimming in seas of rivers
Flowing into me,

I and fish

A Fish and I.

Same different , same.
Water.

An Opportunity

I climb the winding stair to the landing on the second floor.
I pause, anticipating new life lessons on this day
Then quietly opening the door,
I see her.

She is propped on several large pillows against a massive ornate headboard.
I am greeted with a smile and open arms ready for a hug
Strewn over her bed are tools for art making
Tools for child's play,
Oil paint sticks in every hue, soft pastels, paper and pencils too.
Rags for turpentine, a roll of tissue for blending colors,
 As she paints her life, the good times and the dismal.

Nothing escapes her scrutiny; images filled with skulls and
Masks of death's foreboding presence hang on the walls.
Sitting in bed she offers coffee perking on the kitchen stove and
Soon we are immersed in our work as, teacher/mentor, student /artist, friend
and confidante alike.
Exchanging colors sharing whatever the other needs and doesn't have.
I, a cobalt blue, she a cadmium red as we balance and harmonize our efforts

I move from the foot of her bed to rearrange pillows, offer another coffee.
She declines, instead decides she will get out of bed.
She grips my hands as I steady her weight and a few steps she is able to take.
Thus we spin the day one step at a time,

She struggles with her pain and I with mine.
Today she finishes a painting and it seems
Joy lights her face like a sun beam.
Her pain subsides replaced with determination to fight
Isolation, fear, immobility and frustrations of a grave illness.

Integrity is key to survival for it is true
The word artist means to do,
She paints life not always beautiful but from her point of view.
Cancer sucks her strength, pain keeps her in bed
Under medical onslaught she refuses to bend
Certain she will transcend.
"Every obstacle is an opportunity to learn,
 To grow and strengthen resolve," she says.

To raise ideals in the midst of reflection transcending victimization.
We honor what she shared.
The life of an artist, vessel for visualization.

In the woods

We live in a crooked house
That sways and swings,
Creaks, crooks and cracks
All day.

A crooked house with
Crooked people living crooked ways
In crooked rooms that swing and sway
With furniture that is broken and fixed
In styles of various periods, painted and mixed.
Beds lean as they dip
 Floors need rugs so you won't slip
Or run the risk of breaking a hip…

Mornings in this crooked house
Develops crooked backs and bones
Before the house straightens itself
With creaks and groans
It settles into winter's bitter cold,
 Of icy rivers made by
Sunbeams melting snow.

Stepping Out

Stepping Out

"Stepping Out" is the result of an exercise developed to build strength in the hand, a part of my instruction under the mentorship of Maestro Francisco Espinoza while I was a student in Burgos Spain.

It involved holding several brushes loaded with paint between the fingers, using equal pressure to create an image. I did many successful paintings using this technique!

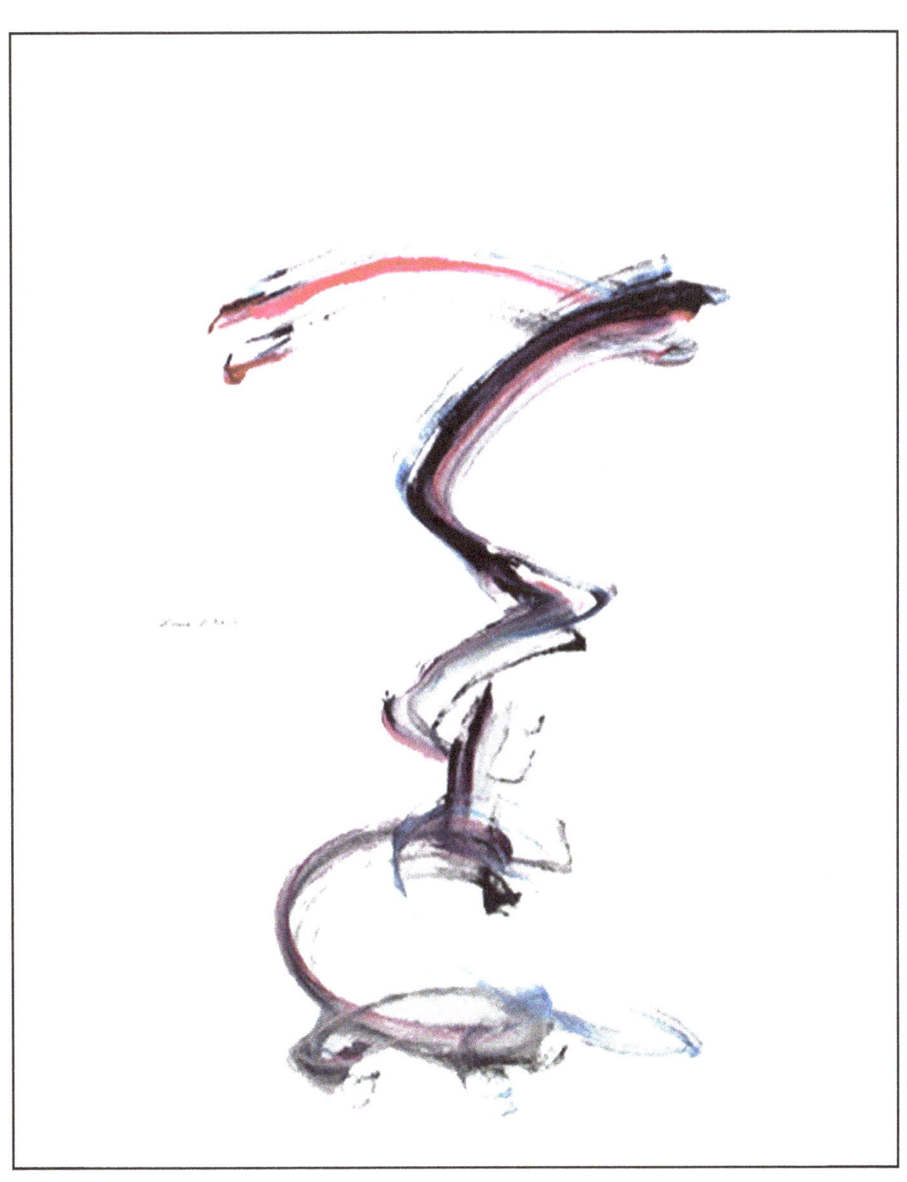

Stepping Out”

55” H x45“ W

Acyrlic on wood

Freedman

I saw a freed man today

Feeling his way

As he stepped along

Tapping his dark and silent song

Step along, step along

As if day were night and night were day

Stepping alone

Cane in hand

Marching to a band of tooting horns and screeching tires.

He strides with cane in hand,

A freed man, head high, smiling, a look beyond sight

Strolling down the center of an inner city's street,

Midst frantic rush hour traffic and

Burning exhausts' heat.

A free man with white cane in hand.

Tapping to an encore band.

Ode to Ginsberg

Da   Da DaDa

Da Da Da Da

Daaah Da Daaah Da Da

In the distance

I hear him playing an ancient instrument

Chanting Yiddish preludes that will

Open our ears

For a wonderful poem about

"Sitting, Buddha."

Da Da Dada

Democracy

Democracy demands its own season.
As validation to wage a war,
Equality is hailed as the reason.

To disagree is judged as treason
For which one could be burned in tar.
Democracy demands its own season.

Two brothers were drafted for the legion.
Two sons she lost in a land afar.
Equality is hailed as the reason.

One refused to kill and was undone
Following horrors grossly bizarre.
Democracy demands its own season.

The other son pointed his weapon
At his infantry leader's three striped bar.
Equality is hailed as the reason

For my brothers' deaths and Mama's sons
Are now in heaven, each a shining star.
They died in a war that wasn't won.
Democracy has its season.

Changing Guard

When pilgrims land uninvited,
Natives become strangers
In
A new world order.
Democracy reigns
And there is equal enslavement for all.
In
The new world order
Natives become strangers,
Disenfranchised,
Disoriented,
Uprooted,
Transported,
Forgotten,
And starved to death by equal nutricide!

BALM IN GILEAD

Through political strategy, the dye was cast
 He became the healing balm.
His smile did the work like magic.
A potent potion to soothe America,
A nation wounded in trust and punished by greed.

A balm created by those who write the book on
How to use the tone, the texture, and color of a balm.
The dream team concocted "Mr. President" Barack Obama
A media personality, a concoction with celebrity presence.

Embellished with palliative words to soothe,
Endowed with a Jamie Fox smile, a Denzel swagger and
A combination of all the features of popular black male film stars.

Tossed into the sewage,
 A country's ideals
By makers of the laws that fill books of
Engaging demonic magic, spells, enchantments and concoctions

Invented to spare us from sewage?
"Who, who, who" prescribed this salve?
Better to reek of sewage …
Than smell of pollution's stench.

Move: A Tragedy of Errors

Part One: The Children Couldn't Move

In the bunker
The children were put
For protection
From flying bullets,
To be safe from drowning
By the onslaught of the
Firemen's water hoses.

Atop the roof
In the bunker
They hid…
For protection.

They were the first to die.
Their bodies tossed,
Parts dispersed like missiles
Targeted far beyond.
For they dared not move
As they cowered there,
Crouched in the bunker.
Their hiding place was a target for the bomb,
Was the first hit.
Now we all admit
When life is the target-
Children die
As governments drop bombs.

Part Two: The Move to Die

Time.
Time to Move.
Move man, man move!
It's hot as hell.
Move!
Open the door
Can't take this heat anymore!

Let me outa here! Don't shoot!
We're coming out, we're burning up

But the government fired
The sound echoed,
Then ricocheted.

The deaths
Long since bought.
Thus the signers are now paid.
Death inscribed and paid for
By nonconformity.
That death eludes
All differences
Is truth's reality.
As real as governments
By people pay
When bombs descend
On transformation day.

Part Three: The Fire Moves

The fire
Moved,
Once coaxed to burn.
Sweeping like a sucking vacuum
Devouring houses
Full of furniture and items of endearment.
Houses consumed
Stone collapsing
Wood disappearing
Bricks dismantling
Papers burning
Plastic melting
The fire ate hungrily
Its appetite soaring.
Feeding on
Memories…
Memories of fear
Memoirs of hatred

Contiuued next page

Fashioned by ideologies
Revived in violence
And inhuman deeds.
The fire moved
Powerful and strong as truth manifested,
Fueled by distrust
Invited by prejudice
Coaxed by fear
Nudged by anger
Encouraged by hatred.
Leaving behind:
Ashes
Ashes of lives
Ashes of hate
Ashes of fear
Ashes and death
Leaving ashes, rocks
Mortared stones,
Dismembered bodies.
Ashes of a government
By the people,
For the people.
The fire,
Its spirit freed-
Moved on
To forests and…
Other homes…
In other places…
Ignited by an infestation of bombs
Avenged by nature's
Mudslides, forest fires and floods across a nation!

Larch

Larch

The characteristics of the Larch tree or Tamarack inspired this image. It belongs to the genus of the coniferous trees. Coniferous trees generally remain green year round and decorate many homes during the Christmas season.

However, the Larch turns a brilliant Hansa yellow in the fall and by winter its branches are bare and nubby. The bright yellow needles cover slopes of mountains finding their way into streams and valleys below. It is deciduous and coniferous. Like Hansa yellow, it embodies the duel ying-yang phenomenon.

Larch thrives in adverse conditions and is flexible in winter storms bowing and bending atop mountain peaks. I identify with this hardy and indestructible specimen of nature. It pretty much sums up our journey and how we thrive in spite of the ups and downs in life.

I used my face to portray the concept of mother earth, a metaphor for the many forms of my art, surreal, magical realism, abstract and traditional objectivism.

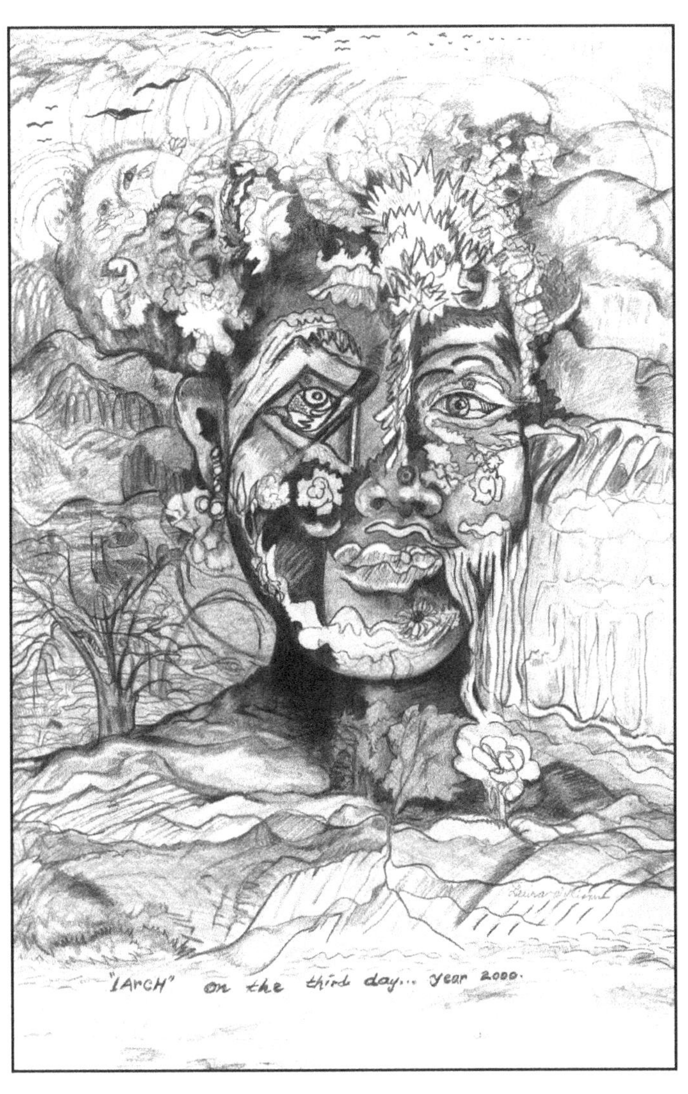# "Larch"

24″ H x 18″ W

Graphite drawing on paper

Friend

You dropped chuckles of smiles on my ears
I nibbled on every sound and each tasted delicious!

I felt your sunshine in my heart and your smile
Stuck in my belly and made it swell with happiness.
My friend, oh love.

I shared the warmth of your embrace
As it spread its healing ray
To those who chose to stay-
Even for a little while.

Yes, strange bodies harbor kindred spirits
For kuon ganjo*
Atop Eagle Peak!

*time without beginning

Once in a lifetime

Once upon a time

There lived a songbird

    On planet earth

Her song vibrated with rivers

    Tuned by oceans, clouds and rain

Her song whispered breezes warm

    And winters frozen

Her voice pitched high over mountains of obstacles

    As she soared, grew wings and sang

Once upon a time, there lived

    Once in a lifetime

Whitney, Whitney, Whitney

        Houston.

CASTING

Fishing for clients, their bodies are bait,
Though assaulted, tormented, abused and afraid.
Standing on corners they watch and they wait.

Does it matter if they are gay or straight?
A trick's ultimate goal is to be laid.
Fishing for clients, their bodies are bait.

Daily they sell their soul at the pimps' rate.
Most often abused before they are paid,
Standing on corners they watch and they wait.

They think of their pimp as their true soul mate
Fearfully, throughout this nightmare they wade
Fishing for clients, their bodies are bait.

Sad, blank eyes reflect a pitiful state
For these unemployed there is no financial aid.
Standing on corners they watch and they wait

For husbands who betray the wives they hate,
Trapped in the web of the policeman's raid.
Fishing for clients, their bodies are bait
Standing on corners they watch and they wait.

SISTER ANNA MARY- ANNE MARIE

Sister Anna Mary
  I met
While packing some portraits away
"You look like an Anne Marie",
I said.
"No", the picture replied.
"My name's Anna Mary,
I'm not Anne Marie."
Strange, I thought
That a portrait could talk
I put the sketch away
Again, I heard it say,
"Sister Anna Mary, I'm not Anne Marie."

Strange I pondered
As I pedaled my bike to my
First yoga class.
Strange that a picture could speak,
Speak with words to me.

I approached the building
And entered tentatively
The door flung open and there she stood
Sister Anna Mary
Angel Anne Marie.

"Come in", she said with outstretched arms
And led me to my seat.
With gleeful eyes
And glad replies,
"So happy you've come,
You're in for quite a treat."

The Larch

I am concerned

 About the depiction of women as insignificant

 Pounds of flesh

With boobs that shake

And butts that wiggle-

Commercial as the latest soda pop ad.

Fizzling, fragile, fizzle.

As fragile as a bubble on a bar of soap!

For a woman's strength lies not in her bosom

Nor in the firmness of her buttocks…

Her softness is beneath the surface

Of her flesh

And it penetrates the depths of her soul.

Strong and soft, flexible, bending, stretching

Controlling, strong, soft, flexible

She encompasses

The spectrum of life

In her being.

Strong and sturdy, bold and unadorned,

In winter she braces her arms like

The branches of a tree.

Bending, bracing, bowing

Against the bitter, cold, reality of

Stark rejection and perverse affection.

While sucking and sucking and sucking

Like the thirsty seed she is,

She becomes enlightened by the melting snow

As she quenches her thirst

And grows and grows,

In the winters of her life.

As yet she feeds the embryo of her mind

And another ring of wisdom

Is added to her trunk.

From warm, soft and fluffy white

Pink, pastel-like petals of lace

To firm expanding buds of promise.

Promising harvest,

Harvesting.

Fruitful

To feed, to nourish

Continued next page

The entity of life

A nourishing of hope.

Her strength is like a tree whose beauty

Changes to fit the season,

Green and refreshing

Providing

A calm, shady embrace in the heat of

The passionate summer of life.

At once!

She bursts into a fiery full blown mass of energy

Displaying her beauty for

 The world to gape at…

She spreads herself like a brilliant carpet

For children to skip through

And men to gather up;

For her sisters who have long been

Chopped down,

To be remembered for what they were

Warm and golden, cozy brown and crunchy mellow

Like Leaves, mounds of leaves.

Different shapes—different sizes, many hues, varied colors.

Warm and nice

Vibrant and fiery—

A log for winter…

Everlasting…

Ancient…

More beautiful with age.

Under Cerulean Skies

Under Cerulean Skies

Poppies proliferated on the plateaus of the Swiss mountains when I visited there one summer. The meadows glowed crimson even at night when cerulean skies became Prussian blue. Their glow spread out across meadows in the moonlight.

I painted images of poppies. I separated their petals and studied the forms. I designed motifs with seed pods and when I came home, I planted them in my garden. They inspired a body of work entitled "In the Field." This painting expresses my love of nature, the land, water, plants, all life.

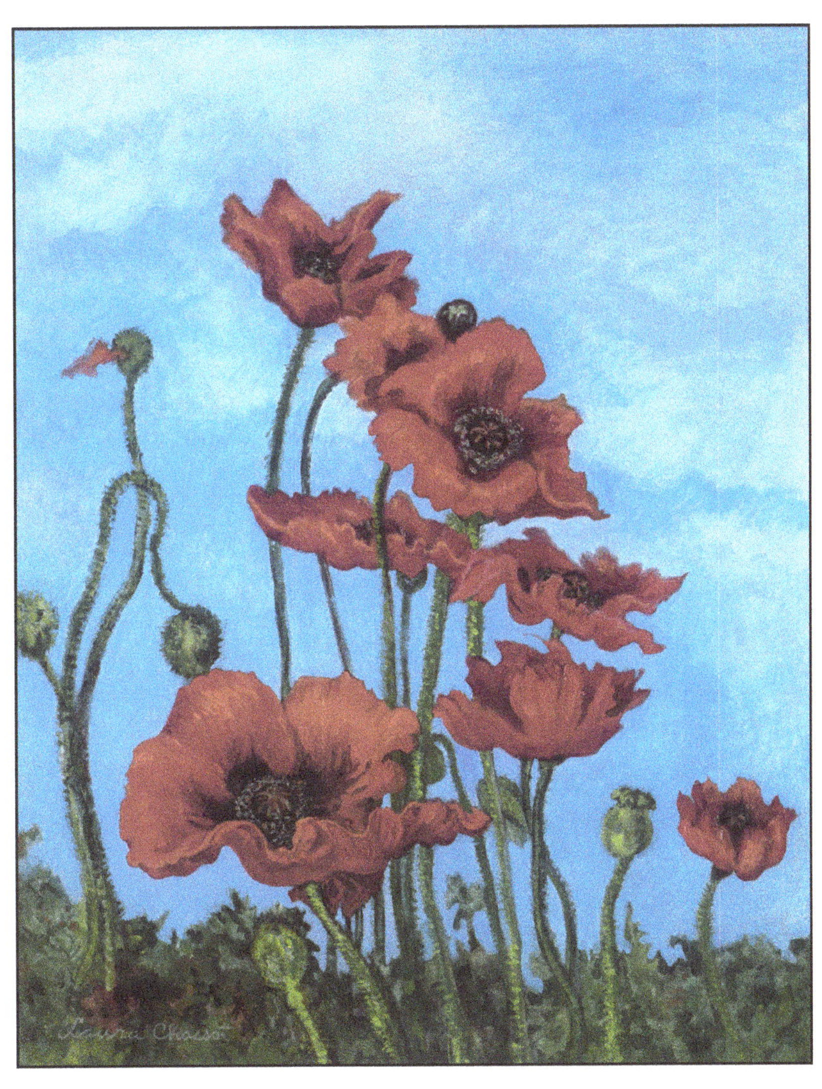

"Under Cerulean Skies"

36″ H x 24″ W

Acrylic on canvas

Wildflower

Your flamboyant beauty
Declares itself to field and meadow alike.

With roots deep and strong you burst through
Icy cold and hardened earth.
Defying winter's bitter snow,
Deprivation, cannibalistic drought and parasitic manifolds.

Wildflower, withered now,
You embrace freezing winds and brutal storms.
Still, spring will see you breakthrough…

Bold and showy once again
For you know
How the sun shines
After winter's cold.

Wildflower budding
Energized and sensuous
Reborn to herald another season of joy!
Announcing the glory of spring.

Releasing Power

Sun pierced clouds float above crowds

Sun beams on my temple emanating light

Releasing power

Relieving

Restoring

Renouncing cold, bitter ice shimmering icicles

Hanging from shingles

Dangling in

Sunshine's prism of ice

Revising smoky shadows

Curved in shades of Bluebirds,

Stripes of flags in blue, white,

Branchedgraggling bright

Dove gray

Blended with yellow

Perched

With moss seasoned

Graggly gray, dove blended with yellow

Sunlight

Creeps

Between trees and skies

Clouds

Shadows

Slanted

Blinds

Windows

Prisms

Faceted across the bright red walls of a cardinal's yellow beak.

RYE BEACH

Exploring density of line
As waves rush the beach
Patterns emerge and stalks of algae
Ride on the bubbly fringes of morning.

First Snow

With white paper, ruler, scissors,
I make a magic square.

I fold not once but thrice to create a Magic triangle.
I crease the folded edges so it turns out crisp and nice!

Cutting between each fold, turning scissors in and out
I make a dozen or more.

 I watch them flow from my hand like God's.
 Paper snowflake images, artistic delights

They fall and land –
On my desk, on the floor

What a mess, what a mess!
Snowflakes everywhere

I tape them on windows, doors, even walls.
Outside, live snowflakes fall on cars, people, and houses,

Kissing streets and pavements with Ivory soap shavings,
Making our world appear clean and neat.

White paper, blank.
White snow, blanketing.

Flakes.
First snow falls.

Fall Journey

I like the softness of fall

A billowy bird-like cloud twixt Summer and winter.

Blended edges and muted hues

Undiminished softness.

Raw sienna, cadmium flashes of yellow gold.

Great eyes of bridges, gaping cities

Burnt sienna fall.

Bridges, reflections, trees naked and drying.

CLING CLANG!

Cling clang

Motors hum,

Stalagmites shimmer, sparkle, glitter reflecting,

Against cerulean skies

Swish of doors

Rattling, shaking passengers from train to train.

Hum, hum click clack clang clang train stops.

CENTRAL STATION!!

I like the softness of fall

No smoking on the train

Yellow edged balconies looking down the track…

WARNING! Get back, get back.

In London, mind the line, mind the line.

Underground fall, soft warm wools replace crisp cottons.

Crepe paper streamers creep across a cobalt sky

Fading reds and yellows, mutual melon orange.

Subdued fall.

Journey of the Goddess

She rose from the hot rays of a sunrise and gave us light
Flowing into sunsets' purple hues and singing the blues of
midnight
Dawning with dew drenched vapors of mythical rites
Eve avowed mystical powers expanding, imploding life's
energy, exploding.

Before the energy of Eve's light there was
No man, no god in sight.
She was severed from the earth and creative energy surged
A powerful essence scent of goddess was that, when Eve
emerged.

Eve sowed the reaping of her soul
And planted the seeds of life with a thought I'm told.
Gave birth to witnesses, her first born, eternal tree of life
everlasting with
Roots stretching underground protected by dreams of self.

Nourished by seeds proliferated by her deeds alone
Creator of the first human clone.
Creative Eve energy of all time, birthing first thought in our
mind, goddess
Reaping reproduction's mysteries, cut, ripped, pulled and
coaxed from earth

slandered by androcentric texts throughout the ages
Her creative power reviled and feared by priests and sages
Cited as a paradigm of evil and destruction

Betrayed by lust and seduction of lesser gods
Eve is still Eve regardless of her name
Mother of humanity one and the same
Keeper of the seed of life and vessel of the soul
Goddess, creator of life before man imagined the creation of
god.

Goddess, once honored by children and man
Worshipped before our time began
Goddess, disenfranchised, disrespected, slandered and
burned at the stake
These acts demonstrate an effort to dismiss and diminish

Powers natural to the feminine
Will these acts be thrust aside
When peaceful order is returned to her domain
And there is no longer a need for gain?

Specialization

Ravished by scarlet fever, polio, syphilis, gonorrhea and
now aids…
We live a Frankenstein realty
A Frankenstein realty where diseases are created to fit the
crime
 Of drugging and poisoning our society.

Poisoning society in the guise of alleviating pain
While creating fear, magnifying pain
And causing more pain
Poisons disguised as cures for newly invented ills mani-
fested as disease.
While making incurable
An onset of new dis- eases created to fit the strategy of
new drug wars
For society's dependency on new drugs
We suffer under capital's credo,

Leave no body intact, recast parts.
Leave no body, mind, psyche whole and well or capable
of functioning.
Ravish every digit on every hand
Replace bones destroyed by prescription
Implant cow matter to anchor teeth and
Chips to tick like our clocks

Valkyrie

Like the Valkyrie named Mist, riding through the air and over water

Deciding who will live and who will die,

Unheedful of the lover's cry.

This blinding fog heralds love,

 invading space unprotected beneath our ribs.

Hearts are victims penetrated by cupid's piercing arrows,

 A target for love's dart.

Love, a blinding haze, obscuring vision with clouds that daze,

Mist hovers, dimming senses, confusing, hindering all

power of discernment.

Love leaves us without choice.

It chooses us

 Like Mist, the Valkyrie of ancient Norse myths.

Fire

Hot heat burning warmth
Glowing soft
Bright light
Cold yellow warm
 Fireflies gathered in waves.
I retreat
Inside a quiet place
Cold, alone
Away from
Black coals burning
Red fire heat and
Yellow warm
Hot heat passions,
In a time I die again
Inside running
Away from feelings
Which carry me to the zone

Where no one can touch
The well
 is dry
I shut doors tight locked-
And walk among the dead, disillusioned,
Disenfranchised, dismembered.

In a time I glowed red hot,
Yellow fire
Black coal singing singed passion
Heat hot touching inside feelings
Metaphoric embryonic desires
Reaching deep
Touching lustful, laughter and pain,
Embracing joy, accepting sorrow in
Ignoble bliss,

I burned.
Red hot radiating life
 I glowed burning with wonder
In love with life's fire
White heat blue flamed
Hot, heat burning.
I live, unafraid of
Consumption.

Awe

And yes some are known by their good works

Which reap havoc and confusion

Birth via virgin

Death on a cross

Thou shalt not kill,

 Empower

Pilate's hand.

Deemed grossly certifiable

Clinical as

Society's gate keepers

Would phrase…

This act of violence

These acts of violent rejection of

Terms .

This act of equalization

A tip on the balance scale

Want or need is it worth pursuing?

Only I decide for me

A choice is grand for now.

I understand on the bottom rung at the top of the ladder

It is life which is profound.

The wizard in us all

Evoking miracles and magic

Transposing, transferring, transplanting seeds

Among   each   one.   We. All.

Island Fantasy

Island Fantasy

Monochromatic blues and white representing water, waves, sky and vacation dreams on the ocean were miraculously manifested when I posted a photo of an island vacation on my bulletin board.

An avid collector saw this painting in an exhibit and called it "Island Fantasy." It reminded her of her vacation home.

When I revealed that I had not been to the islands, I was invited to vacation with her and her friends who had homes in St. Martin! For me, it was an example of the power of focused visualization.

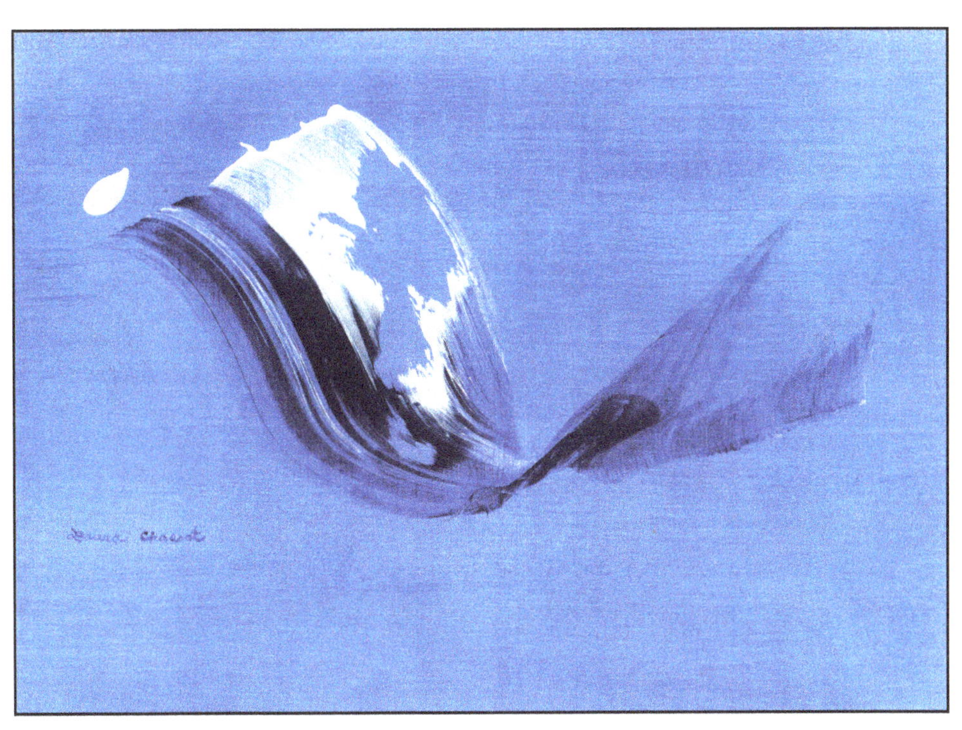

"Island Fantasy"
19″ H x 21″ W
Acrylic on paper

Lazy Mornings

Face down

Lazy Morning

Breakfast in bed

Food on a silver platter.

Champagne on Sunday,

Lazy morning.

Face down.

Omen

I am weed
Growing along roadsides
    leaving scents of flowering thought.
I am pollen riding on air
 Permeating
     dreams
 I look
 Overhead
 A black cloud of crows
Swoop the cornfield.
An omen.

I'm too young to know an omen
When black clouds flow over
Cornfields.
Swooping
Devouring
Leaving stalks
Barren.

I'm too young to know
Omens
As I watch preacher
Pointing gun into the sky
 Whenever black clouds fly.

Recalling,
Black clouds dropping from the sky—
 Omens.
 Growing like weeds
Along life tracks,
 On roads and scented
 Fields below hills and mountains.

Miracles

Rocks spin soil for Gaia

As sacred beings, frightened beings weep blue moons

and

Lilac lifeboats boot over rocks unfolding inner miracles

Of warm, mild and juicy successes

Cooking like Groucho Marx on the gingko farm!

Art is A Religion

Pesto days are gone and I am alone—

Creating stories

Worded by thoughts of

"Pesto" days,

French "bred" and

Wine's sophisticates

For

Art is a religion,

The practice is creation

The Red Flag

Red is

Primal

Origin

Energy

Of courage, life's beginning

Source of

Warmth,

Excitement and

Emotive

Earthen clay.

The matador

Waves the red

Flag of courage

And the

Great bull

In excitement

Fury and confusion, charges

 In

Confusion.

The great bull

Is slain.

Talk of the Town

We talked

And walked

Promenading by the sea.

We ate

And slept

And dreamed in harmony.

We painted the town

Right side up,

Then turned it upside down!

Together–

In love

WORDS

Words are conceived to deceive

Like jesters before the court

Words occulted

Words twisting,

Turning, Yearning

To be

Alive

To live

Conceived to deceive.

Words.

Forked.

Tongue-tied words

Mountain City

Mountain City!

Mountain City is my languid soul's cry

Mountain City before I die…

I see mountains close to the eye

Touching the sides as we swished by

Where every child grew

Within sight of the Blue Ridge peeking through.

Hazy, clouded brush stroke hues of mountain humps

Smiling back at you!

Perfume of mountain brew…

Lazy on the wind—

I smell it now, unchanged,

As I view Mountain City hills of stone…

Pickled eggs and honey-cone,

Larch trees vying for sun

And clover meadows where children run.

Mountain City!

Mountain City!

My languid soul's cry

Mountain City's tater—pie!

On Responsibility

No one's head rest on me.
No one's grief,
No one's pain,
No one's guilt
    Nor joy
      Or shame.
For no one's head
Am I to blame –
No responsibility I
For any one's dream
Stolen, lost or found.
To no one's vision am I bound.
No one's head
    nor destiny
Rest on my shoulders
'cept for me.
 No one white
    nor black
    nor lost
No one ill
    Or faint
Can toss this inner self
'cept for me.
Pilate's hands I needn't wash
Nor fight with people
For those things lost are forever found
    or never sought
     when stolen
      and trodden to the ground.
No one's head rest on me.
No one's destiny
But my own.

For on my shoulders all alone
Rests no one's head but
 My own.
Thus through the mystic
I must clear
Entangled masses of shame, poverty and pain…
Looking through my life
For someone
       some thing
       some god
         to blame—
For the blackness
   that's made my greatness,
Mistakes are precious healings to my soul
Where laden pitfalls are offered
Like pots of gold!

My responsibility is to me.
It lies in changing
My destiny.

Forgetting the blame
And using the pain
To power every step
From enslavement's slavery.

Malcolm changed his destiny
Not for me
But for himself
And Martin did the same.
'cause no one's head rest here
But me
And I have
Made my own self free!

Roots

(for Aunt Ret)

For the children said she…

That's the way I want it to be.

Tradition for the children

And seasoned folks like me!

Not lost in herself,

Though to others it might seem.

For she knew that history is the beacon our children beam…

So I say for the children,

That they may see

History in you and me.

For the Children,

They must know the best from me to thee.

Our course in them we vest.

For the Children,

Got to start them off right—

For they be our brightest sight.

For the future I say

For all eternity—

Enlighten their spirits

With the best from you and me!

I like Me

83

There is no one I would rather be, than me.

And therein lies the problem; I am.

I don't want to be like God, family, a race, or saint, whoever.

Not Mohammed either.

Would I want to dream like King?

Dreams foster nightmares,

I am aware, awake, not blind, can see.

I like my reality

The one I've created for

Me.

I am somebody at peace, who loves

Being in my skin, in my world, in harmony,

You see.

I like me.

About the Author

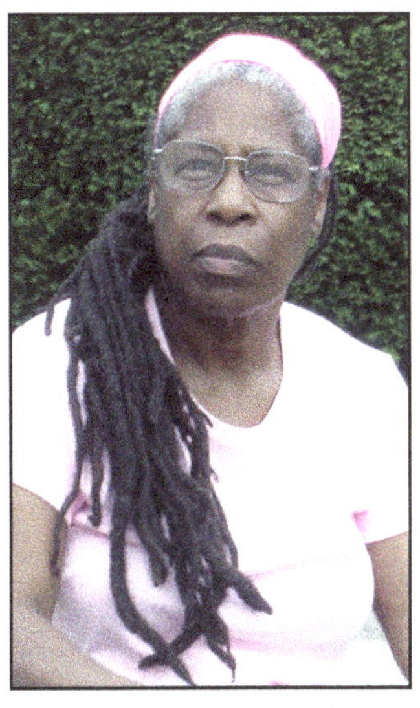

Author photograph by Emmanuel J. Chassot

Laura Williams-Chassot is an award winning artist with exhibitions to her credit on both sides of the Atlantic in the United States and in Europe.

Laura uses a language to describe her paintings and process similar to a physicist or priest. She believes that energies in the universe can be channeled to create specific forms with a single "stroke". Laura's broad based scope includes studies in music, poetry and painting. Her approach to art is that there are relationships between all of its forms. Her work is part of the permanent art collection at the MD Anderson Cancer Center at Cooper in Camden, NJ.

She conducts workshops for all ages in painting and poetry, throughout Philadelphia and the surrounding area. Laura currently resides in Collingswood, NJ.